RSPCA

All About...

Dogs and Puppies

Fun facts and tips about your pet

SCHOLASTIC

Contents

Each year, thousands of unwanted dogs and puppies are re-homed by the RSPCA.

This book has been created to help you to give your pet dog or puppy a happy, healthy life. Read on and find out all about dogs and puppies.

Quick quiz

How much do you know about dogs and puppies? Take this true or false quiz to test your doggy know-how. Then turn the page and read on to find out more about these amazing animals and if you've got what it takes to be a responsible dog owner.

1 Dogs don't have a very good sense of smell.

2 An indoor kennel or dog crate can be used to discipline your dog.

3 Puppies can normally leave their mother at eight weeks.

4 You can train your dog to tell you if it needs the toilet.

5 Dogs can be trained to assist people with mobility issues.

Answers

1 False. Turn to page 44 to find out more about doggy senses. **2** False. For more on dog crates, turn to page 64. **3** True. **4** True. Turn to page 68 to find out more about toileting. **5** True. Find out more about assistance dogs on page 32.

Meet the canine family

Dogs are part of the canine family. They are furry, four-legged animals with sharp teeth and wagging tails. Some people wrongly believe that dogs are wolves in disguise. In fact, pet pooches are very different from their wild cousins, which include wolves, dingos, coyotes and jackals. It has taken thousands of years for dogs to become the pets we know today.

Did you know?

It's official – dogs are definitely a person's best friend. It has been found that people who have pet pooches are generally happier and healthier than those who don't.

Four woof-tastic first canine facts

1. The first canine cousin, Hesperocyon, lived in North America around 40 million years ago. It had short legs, a long nose and a long tail, and looked more like a mongoose than a dog.

2. Borophagus looked more dog-like, with massive jaws and teeth. It prowled the plains of North America about 10 million years ago.

3. Dire wolves lived in North America during the last Ice Age. These prehistoric predators were bigger than any wolves today, and preyed on mammoths and other large mammals.

4 All pets dogs are descended from wild grey wolves that first lived about 300,000 years ago. The posh scientific name for a wild wolf is Canis lupus.

Doggy cousins

Wolves, coyotes, jackals and dingos are close cousins to dogs. Take a snap and you'll see some similar family features, especially their pointed ears and canine teeth, but they behave in very different ways to pet pooches. Time to meet the Canids...

Wolves

Wolves are the largest members of the family, reaching more than 1.5 m long. The biggest and furriest wolves live in chilly parts of Canada, Alaska and Russia. Wolves hunt in teams. That way, they can prey on moose, deer and other animals that are much bigger than themselves.

Coyotes

Coyotes live in North America. They're famous for not being fussy eaters. In fact, they'll chomp on anything they can get their teeth into. This includes animals, such as rodents, fish, frogs, snakes and insects as well as fruit and vegetables.

Jackals

Jackals are slender and speedy with long legs for running fast after their prey. They live and hunt in pairs, and usually stay together for the whole of their lives. You can track down jackals in Africa, and some parts of Europe and Asia.

Dingos

Dingos live throughout Australia and in south-east Asia. They are found in deserts, mountains and forests. At dawn and dusk, they set off in search of food. In Australia, their favourite meal is kangaroo – if they can run fast enough to catch one.

Did you know?

Wild dogs have to find their own food.
Your dog relies on you to feed and care for it.

Five WILD wild canine facts

5 Wolves are famous for howling, although they don't actually howl at the Moon. They do it to talk to other wolves in the group. Howling also warns wolves outside the group to stay away from their territory.

4 The raccoon dog looks different to the rest of the dog family. In fact, it hardly looks like a dog at all. It has long, thick fur and black markings on its face – just like a real raccoon.

3 The raccoon dog is the only dog that hibernates. It scoffs loads of food in autumn, then settles down in its burrow and lives off its fat through winter, waking up again in spring.

2 The smallest member of the dog family is the cat-sized fennec fox. The fox's most famous features are its HUGE ears. They carry heat away from the fox's body so it stays cool in its desert home.

1 The Arctic fox is brilliant at hide-and-seek. In winter, its fur is white to blend in with the ice and snow. In summer, it turns brown to match the ground.

Four pet pooch facts

4

Pooches are particularly popular pets, with around 10 million in the UK and 78 million in the USA alone.

3 It's thought dogs first became pets around 15,000 years ago. There are many different ideas about how it happened, but it is thought that dogs evolved over many years from wolves that lived at the edges of human settlements. The wolves that were least fearful of humans lived alongside people and gradually became a separate species.

2 Some dogs have been specially trained to help people with autism. They have a calming effect and help with everyday things such as shopping as well as helping autistic people communicate and learn.

1 Dogs can learn the names of their toys. A border collie called Rico has learned the names of 200 toys. He can fetch the correct toy when he is asked to.

Did you know?

Need a name for your pooch?
Here are some of the
most popular...

● Boys...
1 Max
2 Buddy
3 Charlie
4 Sam
5 Jake

● Girls...
1 Bella
2 Daisy
3 Lucy
4 Molly
5 Maggie

Three top dogs in myth and legend

Laelaps and the Teumessian fox

A Greek myth tells of the never-ending chase between Laelaps, a magical hunting dog who always caught his prey, and the Teumessian fox, who could never be caught. In some versions, Zeus ended the chase by turning them to stone. In others, he placed them in the sky as two constellations Canis Major and Canis Minor so their chase continues forever across the heavens.

Jackal god

The Ancient Egyptian god, Anubis, was often shown as a man with a jackal's head. He was god of the dead and mummification. When mummy-makers began work on dead bodies, the chief always wore a jackal mask to stand for Anubis.

Three-headed guard dog

Greek and Roman myths tell of a monstrous, three-headed dog, Cerberus, who guarded the gates of the Underworld. He only allowed the dead to enter but never let them leave. In Roman mythology, the hero Orpheus, sneaked past him. Orpheus played beautiful music that sent Cerberus to sleep.

Dogs of books, films and TV

For years, dogs have dazzled in books, films and on TV. Ready for some four-footed star spotting? Here are four top canine celebrities...

Gromit

Gromit is the long-suffering sidekick of Wallace, an absent-minded inventor, in a series of stop-motion animated films created by Aardman. The pair have many adventures together, thanks to Wallace's wacky inventions, with clever Gromit often coming to his owner's rescue.

Lassie

The film *Lassie Come Home* tells the story of Lassie, a collie dog, who is sold to a new owner but manages to escape. She survives many dangers, including being dognapped, to find her way back home. The part of Lassie was played by a dog called Pal.

Pongo and Perdita

Pongo and Perdita star in *101 Dalmatians,* a Disney film based on the novel by Dodie Smith. The pair have 15 puppies who, along with many others, are stolen by the wicked Cruella de Vil. Pongo, Perdita and their friends set out to rescue them.

Scooby Doo

Scooby Doo is a cartoon Great Dane and TV star. Together with his owner, Shaggy, and friends, Fred, Velma and Daphne, he is part of the Mystery Gang. Their job is to solve mysteries, involving ghosts, monsters and other spooky beings. Scooby is not very brave but he's always hungry, and will do anything for a yummy 'Scooby Snack'.

Three top dogs in history

Seaman

Seaman was a black Newfoundland dog. In 1804, he set off with explorers, Lewis and Clark, on their epic journey across the USA. He travelled thousands of kilometres, despite being stolen and bitten by a beaver. He helped to protect the camp from attack by buffaloes and bears.

Balto

In January 1925, an outbreak of deadly diptheria struck Nome, Alaska. The only medicine was in Nenana, 1,040 km away. Teams of sled dogs were sent to fetch it, braving blizzards and howling winds. Hardy Siberian husky, Balto, led the final push back to Nome.

Robot

In Lascaux, France, Robot the terrier made a fantastic discovery. In 1940, he was out exploring with his teenage owner and friends when he disappeared through an opening in the ground. When the boys explored, they found amazing prehistoric cave paintings that date from about 17,000 years ago!

Did you know?

One of most famous dog-lovers in history is Queen Elizabeth II. She got her first corgi, Susan, for her 18th birthday. Since then, she has owned more than 30.

Dog tails

Dogs don't just stand around wagging their tails or go chasing after balls. Here are some real-life tales of five courageous canines who saved their owners' lives...

Pocket rocket

Zoey, a chihuahua from Colorado, USA, made the headlines in 2007 for rescuing a young child from a rattlesnake. The child was playing in the garden when the deadly poisonous snake tried to strike. Brave Zoey rushed to the snake and attacked it, suffering a bite for her troubles. Luckily, she made a full recovery.

A helping paw

In 2012, a woman living in Nottinghamshire, England, was eating a meal when a piece of chicken got stuck in the throat. Her dog, Sheba, a Japanese akita, was asleep in the kitchen. Sheba woke up, jumped on her owner's back and whacked her with one of her huge front paws. Incredibly, Sheba dislodged the chicken and saved her owner from choking.

Hurricane heroine

Shana saved her owners from death, when they were trapped by falling trees near their home in New York State, USA. The brave dog dug a tunnel under the trees and they were all able to escape to safety. She then kept her owners warm until help arrived.

Diamond dog

In 2011, a pitbull called Diamond, from the USA, won a National Hero Dog Award. She woke her owner, Darryl Steen, to alert him to a fire that was raging through his family's apartment. He pulled one daughter to safety, while Diamond shielded the other under a mattress until they were both rescued.

Barking the alarm

A labradoodle, called Monty, also saved his owner's life in 2012. Maurice Holder from Cornwall, England, was walking by the river when he slipped and fell down a steep ravine. He hit his head and broke several ribs. Eleven-year-old Monty managed to lead his owner back up to safety, then ran to a nearby pub and barked until someone came to help.

Dogs at work

All over the world, dogs go out to work. Some herd animals – cattle, sheep, goats, reindeer and even ducks. They're trained to follow a farmer's voice, whistle or hand signals.

Some top working dogs

- Border Collie (UK)
- English Shepherd (USA)
- New Zealand Huntaway (New Zealand)
- Lapphund (Scandinavia)
- Red Heeler (Australia)

Herding instinct

Some dogs have been bred to help farmers by herding sheep and cattle. The dogs often work as a team to control a big herd or flock. Some dogs run behind to move the animals along, while other dogs steer them from side to side.

Did you know?

In Namibia, Anatolian shepherd dogs are being trained to protect livestock from hungry cheetahs. Before, farmers simply shot the cheetahs, and the cheetahs were dying out. Originally from Turkey, the dogs are big, brave and not bothered by peckish big cats.

Rescue dogs

SAR (search-and-rescue) dogs are specially trained to look for people trapped under collapsed buildings, often after earthquakes and hurricanes, or buried under snow after avalanches, for example. With their brilliant sense of smell, dogs can sniff survivors out. They're also nifty at squeezing into tight spaces. Here's one amazing tale...

On 11 September 2011, terrorists flew planes into the two towers of the World Trade Center in New York, USA. Both towers collapsed, killing and trapping thousands of people. Around 100 SAR dogs helped to look for survivors. A heroic German shepherd dog, Trakr, found the last person to be pulled out alive. He was later rewarded with the Extraordinary Service to Humanity Award from the United Nations – a top honour.

Helper dogs

Some clever canines can be trained to help people who have lost their sight or hearing, or have a disability or illness. Here are just some of the jobs hard-working helper dogs do...

Guide dog

Guide dogs help people who are blind or can't see very well. They guide their owners across streets, on and off buses and trains, and in and out of buildings. Guide dog puppies start their basic training when they're about two months old, going to guide dog training school when they are about 14 months old.

Hearing dog

Hearing dogs work as ears for people who are deaf or have trouble hearing. They are trained to alert their owners if the phone or doorbell rings. They also listen out for danger signals, such as a smoke alarm going off.

Mobility assistance dog

Mobility assistance dogs help their owners with everyday jobs around the home. They're trained to pick things up from the floor, open and close doors, and help their owners get dressed. They can even load and unload a washing machine.

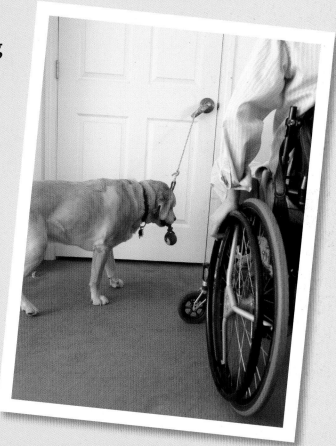

Medical alert dog

Some people with serious illnesses, such as diabetes or epilepsy, can become ill or collapse without warning. Medical alert dogs are trained to tell if this is about to happen. They can then warn their owners that they need to get help.

Dog heroes

Some incredibly courageous canines work with armies, navies and airforces. They go on patrol with the soldiers, helping to protect them and to sniff out deadly bombs and mines.

FACT FILE

Treo

In 2010, a black labrador, Treo, was awarded the Dickin Medal, the UK's top military honour for animal bravery. Treo received his medal for detecting two huge roadside bombs in Afghanistan and saving hundreds of lives.

FACT FILE

Sabi

Another black labrador, Sabi, also worked as a bomb detection dog with the Australian army. In September 2008, she went missing during a battle in Afghanistan and was thought to be dead. Then, over a year later, she was found safe and well by a US soldier. Her handler knew it must be his dog when she ran after her favourite tennis ball.

Did you know?

Dogs also work alongside the police. In 2011, a German shepherd dog, Obi, was sent to help control the crowds during riots in London. He was later awarded an Animals in Action award for his bravery.

Doggy design

Although there are lots of types of dog, many share some similar features. For example, they have four legs, a tail and most have super senses – you can read more about dog senses on pages 44 to 45.

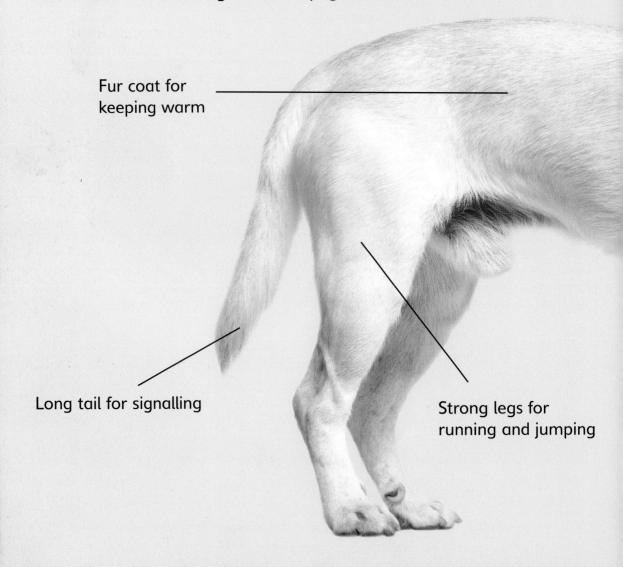

Fur coat for keeping warm

Long tail for signalling

Strong legs for running and jumping

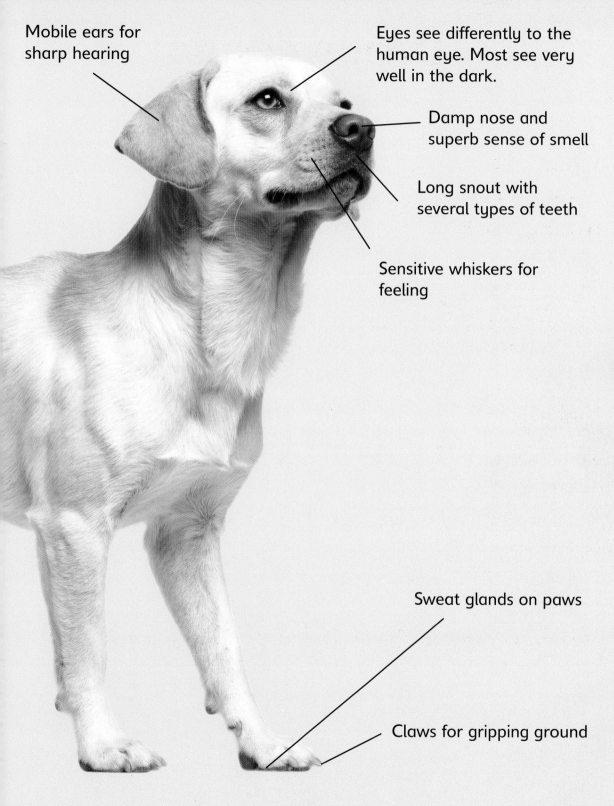

Mobile ears for sharp hearing

Eyes see differently to the human eye. Most see very well in the dark.

Damp nose and superb sense of smell

Long snout with several types of teeth

Sensitive whiskers for feeling

Sweat glands on paws

Claws for gripping ground

All kinds of dog

There are hundreds of different kinds of dogs. They come in different sizes, shapes and personalities. Dogs whose parents and other ancestors belong to the same breed are often called pedigree dogs. They are registered and their family trees can be traced back for several generations. They also have certificates to show they are pure-bred.

Labrador

Labrador retrievers are popular family pets because they can be good-natured and loyal. It is thought that they trace their roots back to Canada, where their ancestors helped pull fishermen's nets ashore. Their fur can be yellow, chocolate (brown) or black in colour. They can be prone to weight gain, which can cause hip problems or make existing problems worse, so, like any dog, owners must be careful not to overfeed them.

German shepherd

German shepherd dogs can have short or shaggy hair, with large, pointed ears. They're strong, can be clever and easy to train, and were once used in Germany to help herd sheep. They are

often used as police and sniffer dogs, as well as being kept as pets. Hip and eye problems can be a problem in this breed.

Boxers

Boxers came from Germany where it is thought they hunted deer and boars. They're big, strong and can be boisterous. They love playing and having fun, and lots of nice, long walks to help burn off all that energy. Boxers can have quite short, turned up noses. This can cause breathing problems in some dogs.

Cocker spaniels

Cocker spaniels are medium-sized dogs, with long, floppy ears and feathery fur. It is thought that they were bred to help humans hunt birds. They've got a superb sense of smell and are often used as sniffer dogs. They can be bright, friendly and gentle. They are prone to ear problems because of their long ears.

Greyhounds

Greyhounds are one of the oldest dog breeds. It is said that thousands of years ago, the pharaohs of Ancient Egypt kept greyhound-type dogs for hunting. With their slender bodies and long, strong legs, they're the speediest dogs on the planet, but they can also make loyal and laid-back pets.

Chihuahuas

Chihuahuas are little dogs that are thought to have originally come from China, although their name is Mexican. Everything about them is minuscule, which means their bones are very fragile so they need very gentle handling. Many chihuahuas enjoy being snuggled up on their owners' laps, but although they are small they still need to do normal dog things like going for walks and running off the lead.

Did you know?

Many dogs don't have family trees. These dogs are crosses between different breeds. They are just as beautiful and can make brilliant pets. They tend to have fewer health problems, too.

Four curious canines

Papillon

The word 'papillon' means 'butterfly' in French. It might seem a funny name for a dog, except this pooch has got long, silky ears, shaped a bit like a butterfly's wings. The papillon also has a long,

furry coat which needs daily grooming. Their small size means their bones are quite delicate.

Shar pei

Shar peis come from China. They've got big heads but small eyes and ears, and curled-over tails. Their coats are thick and wrinkly, as if they're far too big for these dogs' bodies. This can cause skin and eye problems.

Komondor

The Komondor from Hungary has a very unusual coat that hangs down in long, thick cords. It protected the dog from the cold and wolves when it used to work guarding sheep. Its long coat means it can have difficulty seeing properly which could affect how it behaves around other dogs. It needs regular grooming

Chinese crested

The hairless version of the Chinese crested dog has very little hair on its body but it has long tufts on its ears and tail, and furry feet. No wonder this curious canine feels the

cold but also gets sunburnt in summer. It's much kinder and more natural to choose a dog with hair. Chinese crested dogs also have delicate bones, which means they need very gentle handling.

Super senses

In the wild, wolves use their five senses to track down their prey. Pet pooches don't need to hunt for their dinner anymore but their senses are still super–sharp...

1 Sight: many dogs have large eyes that are widely spaced so they can see well to the front and sides. Sight hounds, such as greyhounds, have especially sharp eyes for spotting prey.

2 Smell: dogs can smell much better than you do. Some dogs, such as bloodhounds, have incredibly sensitive noses. It has been found that they have 40 times more smell cells in their noses than you have in yours. Dogs use smell to recognize each other, see page 49.

3 Hearing: have you seen your dog prick up one ear, then the other? It can move its ears to catch sounds from all around. It can also hear much quieter sounds than humans can.

4 Touch: dogs have whiskery hairs on their faces that pick up tiny wobbles in the air made by objects. Their whole bodies are super-sensitive, especially their paws.

5 Taste: a dog can't taste as well as you can – it's got far fewer taste buds. But it can tell the difference between things that taste nasty, and things that taste nice, like juicy meat. Slurp!

Did you know?

A Dobermann Pinscher, called Sauer, once tracked two thieves 160 km across the Great Karoo desert in South Africa... just by following their scent.

Socialization

Dogs are sociable animals who need and love company. If dogs are treated well as puppies they learn to see people as friends and companions. To make sure a puppy grows up to be a dog that enjoys the

company of other animals and people, they must be socialized at a young age. This means that they need to meet plenty of different people, as well as lots of dogs and other animals, especially in the first five to 14 weeks of their lives.

Pleased to meet you!

Puppies that have good experiences meeting lots of different people are less likely to be wary when you handle and approach them. As well as dogs, it is good for puppies to meet other animals. This will help them to settle in a new home if there are other pets living there.

Making sure a puppy is socialized

When you are choosing a puppy, it is helpful to see it playing with dogs other than its mother. It is also useful when you go to a breeder to take along as many members of your family as you can. Watch to see how a puppy responds to other dogs and your family. If the puppy seems nervous or struggles when he or she is handled, this may mean they haven't had enough chances to socialize and could grow up to be scared or anxious, especially around people and dogs they don't know. If you are ever unsure about how well a puppy has been socialized, it is best not to choose them as your pet.

Top tip

Never choose a shy or timid puppy because you feel sorry for him or her, as this may not be the best pet for you and your family.

Doggy talk

Reading the signs

As a dog owner, it is important that you understand and recognize what your dog is feeling so you know how to respond to their needs. Dogs cannot use words to say how they are feeling so they use body language and behaviour to tell others how they feel.

Happy dog

Although many people believe tail wagging always means a dog is happy, it isn't always so. You need to look at the rest of your dog's behaviour. Happy dogs have relaxed faces, and bodies that wiggle from the shoulder backwards.

Your dog might also do a play bow, which mostly means, 'come and play!'. A dog will raise their bottom in the air, and have their front legs flat on the ground. If they have a relaxed face, open mouth and wagging tail it's probably play time!

Did you know?

When you take your dog for a walk, does he or she keep stopping for a wee? This is just one of the many other ways dogs communicate. Your dog is leaving messages for other dogs who can sniff out who's been there before.

If you see your dog doing one or more of the following it may mean they are feeling uncomfortable:

- yawning
- lip licking
- averting their gaze
- turning their head away
- dropping ears
- crouching
- low wagging
- tucking their tail under
- rolling over on their back

If you see these behaviours, your dog needs some space. Always make sure your dog has a quiet, safe place they can go to where he or she is left alone.

If those behaviours do not work, your pet may move on to other ways to try tell you that they are saying, 'keep away!' These can include growling, barking and snapping.

Times when your dog definitely needs some space include when he or she is eating or has food, when your pet has a toy or possession, when he or she is tired or sleeping or feels unwell. Read the signs and be sure to give your dog the space he or she needs at these times and when you see these behaviours. Your pet will approach you when he or she wants to be sociable again.

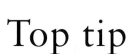

Top tip

If you are concerned about your pet's behaviour, take them to see the vet. He or she will be able to check your dog over to make sure it is fit and well and give you advice. Your vet will be able to put you in touch with a behaviour expert, if needed.

Six dog myths

(1) Dogs can be left in cars

This is a really dangerous dog myth. On a sunny day, the temperature inside a car rises quickly and it can get unbearably hot, even if it isn't that warm outside. Parking in the shade, leaving a bowl of water or the windows open does not keep the car cool enough and won't stop dogs from getting ill, or dying from heatstroke. Never leave your dog in the car – they can overheat in minutes.

(2) Leftovers are fine for a dog

A dog needs a healthy diet, which is balanced and contains all the right vitamins and nutrients he or she needs to stay happy and healthy. Dogs should be given a dog food that is suitable for their age, lifestyle and health, not scraps from your meal, which may contain foods that aren't suitable, or may even be dangerous for your pet.

(3) Dogs can eat chocolate

Chocolate is poisonous to dogs. Always make sure any foods you feed to your pet are made for dogs, or you could make them very ill. Onions and some other human foods are also poisonous to dogs.

4 Dogs can be left at home all day

How long a pet can be left for varies from dog to dog, but they all need regular exercise, company and toilet trips, which means you shouldn't leave them alone for too long. Leaving a dog or puppy can cause them a lot of anxiety, especially if they are not used to being alone. If they chew furnishings, bark a lot or do poos or wees in the house, it's best to ask your vet for advice. They may refer you to a dog behaviour expert.

5 It's OK for a dog to play with sticks

Sticks and branches look fun for a dog to chase, but sharp or splintered edges can damage a dog's mouth or teeth, and if parts of the stick are swallowed it may get stuck in your dog's throat or tummy. For a safe playtime, give your pet a toy that has been designed for dogs.

6 A wagging tail means a dog is happy

While a wagging tail can mean a dog is happy, it can be a warning that a dog is NOT comfortable and may even bite. Because dogs can find it quite hard to tell you how they feel, it is best that you only have contact with a dog when there's an adult around to supervise.

Are you a top dog owner?

Dogs can make brilliant pets but would you make a brilliant owner? Here are some questions to ask yourself if you're thinking of getting a pet pooch.

1 Can you give it a safe, happy and loving home?

2 Can you give it food and water every day?

3 Can you make sure it gets plenty of exercise?

4 Can you play with it and keep it company?

5 Can you care for it for the rest of its life?

6 Can you take it to the vet's if it's ill?

Answers

To be a perfect pooch owner, you need to answer **YES** to every question and many more besides. If you answered **NO** to any of them, think again about getting a dog, as they are a big responsibility and a long-term commitment.

Did you know?

Owning a dog is great fun but it's also a big responsibility. If you own or look after a dog, you must care for it properly and meet all its needs to make sure it is happy and healthy – that's the law.

Picking a pooch

How do you pick your perfect pooch? Do you want an adult dog or a puppy? A puppy is cute and has lots of energy but you'll need to spend time training it. An adult dog may be calmer and have lived in a house before. Do you want a big or small dog? Choose the type and size of dog that fits your family and lifestyle. Once you have decided what type of dog is best for you and your family, here are some things to look for:

Did you know?

If you are choosing a puppy, make sure that you see it with its mother. Puppies should stay with their mothers until they are weaned – have stopped drinking her milk – which is normally around eight weeks of age.

Eyes: clear and bright, with no sign of dirt or soreness

Ears: clean, with no smell or signs of wax inside that could mean ear mites

Mouth: clean, white teeth and pink, healthy gums

Nose: cold and slightly wet

Fur: shiny and soft with no sign of fleas

Legs: strong and sturdy

Bottom: clean and dry under the tail

Behaviour: active, friendly and not afraid

My rescue dog

Giving a rescue dog a home can be very rewarding. If you have decided to adopt a dog, this is how it might happen:

1 Visit your local dog-rescue centre and talk to someone who works there.

2 You tell them about yourself and the sort of dog you are looking for.

3 If the rescue centre feels that you and your family are able to meet a dog's needs you'll meet some of the dogs, then they help to match you with a pet that suits your home and lifestyle.

4 Someone from the rescue centre may come to your house to check it is dog-friendly and to meet the people and any other pets that live there.

5 You collect your new dog and take it home. You may have to make a donation to the centre to cover the costs of caring for your dog while it was with them.

6 A few weeks later, a worker calls to check how your dog's settling in.

Did you know?

In 2012, the RSPCA collected and rehomed more than 194,500 animals. Some couldn't be looked after by their owners any longer. Others were strays, abandoned or cruelly treated.

Essential bits of doggy kit

Before you bring your new dog home, you'll need to get a few things ready. You can buy these bits of kit from a pet shop or rescue centre to make your pooch feel right at home.

Bed or basket:

Your dog will need a cosy, soft bed that they can stretch out in comfortably. Put the bed somewhere warm and quiet where your dog won't be disturbed.

Bowls:

Your dog needs bowls for food and water. Make sure that you wash these every day. Make sure that the amount of food is correct for the size and age of your dog. It is easy to overfeed a puppy if you are using a bowl that's big enough for an adult dog!

Grooming kit:

For keeping your dog's coat in tip-top condition, especially if it's long-haired, see page 72.

Dog toys:

Dogs love toys to chase, chew and tug.

To stop them getting bored, see page 76.

Collar and lead:

The collar needs a tag with your name and
address on, in case your dog gets lost.
You'll need to replace a puppy's collar
as it grows bigger. You will also need
a harness – it's like a doggy seatbelt –
to transport your dog safely in the car.
Make sure it is the right size for your dog
and that it is adjusted correctly for your car.

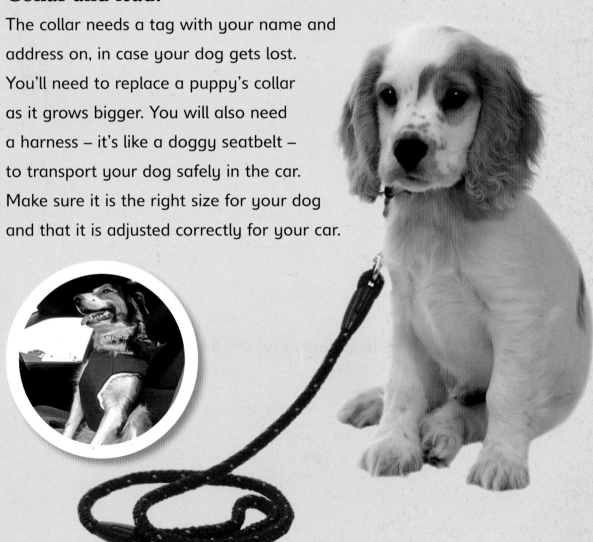

Coming home

Congratulations! The day has come to bring your new dog home. Your pet may be a bit nervous so take things gently at first. It's also a good idea to take a familiar smelling blanket or item for your dog to make him or her feel safe in their new home. Show your dog where its bed is and leave it for a while. You can get big wire pens for puppies where they feel safe until they settle in, see page 64. Put the puppy's bed, food, water and toys inside.

If you've got another dog, let your new pet get to know it slowly. After a while, they should make friends. Give each dog its own bed where it can go for some peace and quiet and make sure they have their own toys and food and water bowls so that they don't compete over them.

Did you know?

Many dogs and cats can live together happily – once they get to know each other. Introduce them slowly and don't leave them on their own together.

Dog-proofing your home

A dog crate, or indoor kennel, is usually made of a wire frame with a tray in which a dog's bedding can be placed. Crates can be used to give your dog or puppy a safe place to go to. They can also be used to help a dog or puppy be left alone, or when it is not possible to supervise them. Here are some do's and don'ts for doggy crates:

Top tip

If you are unsure about how you should use a crate for your dog, ask your vet to advise you.

☑ **DO** make sure that the crate is clean and dry.

☑ **DO** make sure your dog has enough room to stand up, stretch out and turn around.

☑ **DO** place familiar-smelling bedding and toys in the crate for your dog.

☑ **DO** make sure your dog has access to clean, fresh water.

☑ **DO** introduce the crate gradually using positive, reward-based training.

☑ **DO** consider using a crate to transport your dog safely.

☒ **NEVER** use the crate as a punishment for your dog.

☒ **NEVER** place the crate in direct sunlight or in a draught.

☒ **NEVER** leave your dog in the crate for a long time – it should be a safe space for them to go to rather than a place they use all the time.

A dog's dinner

Your dog needs a well-balanced diet to stay fit and healthy. Feed it on special dry or wet dog food. It is generally thought that dry food is better. There are different types of food for puppies, adult dogs and older dogs. You can buy food from a pet shop, supermarket, vet or rescue centre.

Seven tips for feeding time

1 Feed your dog at least once a day. Puppies need several smaller meals.

2 Read and follow the instructions carefully on any dog food that you buy.

3 Make sure your dog always has clean, fresh water to drink.

4 It's important not to overfeed your dog. It may become overweight and unhealthy.

5 Don't feed your dog from the table or give it too many treats.

6 Some human foods, such as chocolate, onions, grapes and raisins are poisonous to dogs.

7 Feeding time can be made fun for your pet by filling a feeding ball or hollow toy with food. Your pet must chew, lick and shake the toy to get at the food, which adds interest to meal times and keeps your pet busy.

Needs must...

Dogs are generally clean animals. They don't like to go to the toilet near their beds so you must make sure your pooch has the chance to go outside to the toilet every few hours. If you get a puppy, it will need to be toilet trained. If you adopt an adult dog they might need some help, too. Your puppy will soon get the hang of things. Here's how...

Take your puppy outside:

- After every meal
- When it wakes up
- After it has been playing or exercising
- When it gets excited
- At least every hour

There are also some tell-tale signs to spot, such as sniffing the ground or walking around in circles. Go outside with your puppy and show it the right place to 'go'. Try to take it to the same place each time. Make sure you reward your puppy or dog when it goes in the right place by giving it a healthy treat, lots of praise and a favourite toy to play with.

Back to school

Training your dog from an early age teaches it how to behave and makes it easier to control. Dogs are fast learners, especially if you reward them with a tasty treat. Never shout at or punish your dog. It won't understand and will only get nervous or scared.

Start off by teaching your dog the basic commands of 'sit', 'down' and 'come'. Always give it lots of praise if it does what you ask it to.

It's a good idea to take your dog along to a training class. This is a brilliant way of spending time with your dog and building a strong bond. Look for a good trainer who only uses reward-based training methods. You can ask your vet, or other dog owners you know for a recommendation. The classes should be fun for your dog, and for you.

Good grooming guide

Keep your dog's coat in top condition by grooming it regularly. This will get rid of any dirt and loose hairs. How often you need to groom your pet varies from dog to dog and should be something to consider when choosing what type of dog to give a home to. If you've got a short-haired dog, groom it once a week. If your dog's got long hair, it will need more grooming.

You might need:

- a bristle brush
- a slicker brush
- a comb

While you're busy brushing, check your pooch's coat for tiny black specks – they're a tell-tale sign of fleas. Ask your vet for some special spot-on treatments to treat your dog, and keep doing this regularly. You may need to treat your dog's bedding and the rest of your house as well.

Did you know?

If your dog rolls in something nasty, like fox poo, it might need a bath. Use a shampoo that's designed for dogs.

Walkies

Does your dog get excited when you pick up its lead? Dogs love going for walks. It helps keep them fit and healthy and stops them getting bored. Take your pooch out at least once a day, rain or shine. The amount of exercise a dog needs depends on his or her age and health. Again, this is something you will need to consider when choosing a pet. Dogs that don't get enough exercise can suffer and become ill.

Doggy keep fit

All dogs need to:
- walk on the lead
- run off the lead – make sure they've learned to come back
- play fetch with a ball
- play fetch with a frisbee

Many dogs also like to:
- do flyball
- do agility training

Did you know?

The fastest dog is the greyhound. It can run as fast as a racehorse. Bet you'd struggle to keep up with that!

DOG WASTE ONLY

Did you know?

When you're out with a dog, make sure you always have poo bags with you. Pick up any dog mess using a bag and put it in the bin. Make sure you wash your hands afterwards with soap, or you might get ill.

Play time

If your dog crouches down on its front legs, and wags its tails or barks, it's probably telling you it wants to play. This is called 'play-bowing'. Dogs love playing with toys, other friendly dogs and you. Make sure your dog has plenty of suitable toys to play with and chew.

Top dog toys

1 **Ball flinger**
Dogs love playing with a ball. A ball flinger can help you to throw a ball further for your dog to fetch.

2 **Chewy bone**
Chewing on a nylon bone is good for your dog's teeth and jaws.

3 **Rubber toy**

It's chewy and bounces when it's thrown for your dog to chase.

4 **Squeaky toy**

Dogs love the squeak but make sure the toy's not too small.

Did you know?

Playing with your dog is fun and helps you to get to know each other better. But don't make your dog play if it doesn't want to. Dogs need their own space sometimes and puppies especially need lots of rest.

Top tip

Always make sure any toy you give to your dog is the right size. If it's too small, they may swallow it and choke. Check your dog's toys regularly for signs of wear. If they are damaged, replace them immediately.

Growing up

Here's how your bouncy puppy grows up into an adult dog...

1 For the first two weeks, most puppies are helpless.
Their eyes and ears are shut and they spend much of their time sleeping and feeding.

2 The puppy's mother helps it go to the toilet by licking its bottom.

3 After two or three weeks, the puppies' eyes open and they begin to explore the world around them and play with their brothers and sisters. They learn very quickly.

4 Just like humans, puppies grow needle-sharp baby teeth. This happens at around three to four weeks of age. By now, they can wee and poo without their mother's help, and will leave the bed to do so.

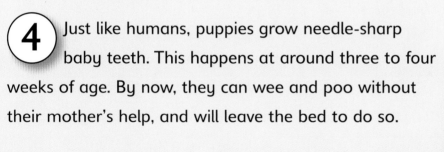

Did you know?

Small dogs may have around six puppies in
a litter. Big dogs may have 12.
In 2004, a Neopolitan Mastiff had a
record-breaking litter of 24 puppies!

5 The puppies learn from their mother, copying her behaviour and movements. They also play with each other and learn the 'rules' of doggy behaviour.

6 This stage is very important for a puppy's development. Gradually introducing puppies to new people, places and noises helps them to become socialized, which is important if they are to become confident, friendly dogs.

7 By around eight weeks, most puppies will be eating solid food and no longer drinking their mother's milk. They will eat several small meals a day. When they no longer drink their mother's milk we say they are 'fully weaned'. Most puppies will then be ready to leave their mothers.

8 At six months, a puppy's adult teeth come in. No surprise that as they are teething they are chewing everything and anything! This is the 'adolescent' stage when a puppy becomes more independent. By now, your puppy's training should be well under way – if you need help training your puppy, ask your vet to recommend a trainer or classes.

9 By the time a puppy is a year old, they count as an adult. Male dogs usually grow bigger than female dogs.

Did you know?

Typically, dogs live for 13 years, but apparently the oldest ever reached the ripe old age of 29 years and five months. He was Bluey, an Australian cattle dog.

Ask a vet

An important part of being a good dog owner is making sure your pet stays healthy. Here are some questions you might want to ask your vet.

Q: How often do I need to take my dog to the vet?

A: Take your dog for a health check a few days after you get it. It will need check-ups every year after that. If your dog looks ill, injured or it is in pain, or if his or her eating habits or behaviour change, ask your vet for advice immediately.

Q: Why does my dog need injections?

A: To stop it getting nasty diseases, such as parvovirus and distemper. A puppy needs its first jabs at around eight and ten weeks. Then dogs need booster jabs every year. If your dog goes to kennels, it also needs a kennel cough vaccine – the medicine is squirted up its nose.

Q: I'm going on holiday. What should I do with my dog?

A: You can leave your dog with a responsible friend or relative. If this isn't possible use recommended kennels. Take your dog's own bed and toys so that it feels at home.

Q: How does microchipping work?

A: A microchip is a tiny chip that fits under your dog's skin. It has a special code, which needs to be registered on a database with your name and address. If a dog is found, the vet can find out who it belongs to by scanning the microchip. Your dog should also wear a collar and identity tag.

Q: Why does my dog need insurance?

A: Pet insurance is always a good idea. If your dog does fall ill, insurance can cover the cost of expensive treatment.

Q: What is neutering?

A: Neutering is a simple operation that prevents dogs from having puppies. This is a good idea because there are many unwanted puppies and it may also help to prevent your dog from getting some illnesses. Your vet can give you more information on this.

Q: Does my dog need dental care?

A: As with humans, keeping your dog's teeth in good condition is really important. If your dog isn't eating, or has bad breath, is dribbling, or their teeth look yellow, take them to your vet. He or she will be able to show you how to care for your dog's teeth.

Common dog problems

Q: What should I do if I think my dog has worms?

A: Dogs can pick up worms from infected food or poo. Then the worms live in their gut and can make dogs, and humans, very ill. Treat your dog every few months with worming tablets or spot-ons which you can get from your vet.

Q: Is it okay for my dog to eat grass?

A: Some dogs like eating grass and it may help them if they have an upset tummy. Grass is usually safe but other garden plants, including sweet peas, foxgloves, daffodil bulbs and rhodedendrons are poisonous to dogs.

Q: How do I know if my dog's got fleas?

A: If your dog is scratching, or you have insect bites on your legs, check your dog's fur for fleas – they look like little black dots. Your vet can prescribe a suitable treatment for your pet.

Q: What things are poisonous to dogs?

A: There are many household things that are poisonous to dogs. Make sure you keep all human medicines and vitamins, cleaning products and slug repellents away from them. Human food, especially chocolate, raisins, grapes and onions will make your dog very ill. If you suspect your dog has been poisoned, take them to a vet immediately.

Dogs quiz

1. Which animals are dogs descended from?
a) jackals
b) foxes
c) wolves

2. When did people first keep dogs as pets?
a) about 15,000 years ago
b) about 20,000 years ago
c) about 5,000 years ago

3. Which dogs hibernate in winter?
a) huskies
b) raccoon dogs
c) labradors

4. In Greek mythology, which dog guarded the Underworld?

a) Anubis

b) Gelert

c) Cerberus

5. Which cartoon dog has its own TV show?

a) Seaman

b) Scooby Doo

c) Theo

6. What are Queen Elizabeth II's favourite dogs?

a) corgis

b) dachshunds

c) great danes

7. What might it mean when a dog looks relaxed, with an open mouth?

a) it's happy

b) it's excited

c) it's cross

8. How long should a puppy stay with its mother?

a) six weeks

b) eight weeks

c) ten weeks

9. Which dog can run the fastest?

a) boxer

b) border collie

c) greyhound

10. How old was the oldest dog?

a) 12

b) 29

c) 8

Answers

1. c), 2. a) 3. b), 4. c), 5. b), 6. a), 7. a), 8. a), 9. c), 10. b)

Dog trivia

1. Some people believe dogs only see in black and white. In fact, they do see in colour, but not quite as vividly as humans.

2. Most dogs have 42 teeth.

3. At the RSPCA's 'Super Sit' event in 2005, a record-breaking 627 dogs took part in a simultaneous 'stay'!

4. Dogs only sweat through the pads in their feet.

5. A dog's sensitive whiskers help it find its way around.

6. Dogs have three eyelids.

7. A dog's wet nose helps it to smell better, as it catches more 'smells' floating around in the air.

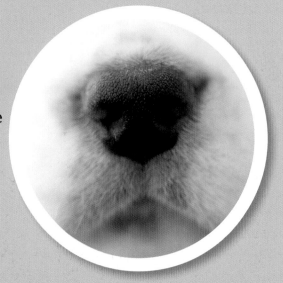

8 The loudest dog bark ever recorded was noisier than a jet flying overhead!

9 In Warsaw, Poland, 700 dogs took part in the largest dog walk in the world.

10 Dogs have sleep patterns similar to humans. If your dog is twitching and moving when it is asleep, chances are it is dreaming!

All about the RSPCA

The RSPCA, or Royal Society for the Prevention of Cruelty to Animals, was founded in 1824 in London. It was the first British animal welfare charity and was originally mostly concerned with the welfare of animals such as pit ponies that worked down in the coal mines. The charity also worked with the hundreds of thousands of animals that served in the military during the First and Second World Wars.

Since then, the RSPCA has worked tirelessly to improve the lives of millions of animals, including those kept as pets and farm animals. It has 170 branches around the country, where staff and volunteers care for the animals that come into the centres. Many are re-homed after they have been nursed back to health and enjoy happiness with their new owners.

By educating people about animal welfare, the RSPCA aims to make sure that all animals live healthy, happy lives and are treated with compassion and respect.

To find out more visit: **www.rspca.org.uk**

Index

Also available